UNWIRED & REWIRED

IT TAKES A CONSCIOUS DECISION TO BE HAPPY

A METHODICAL APPROACH TO UNWIRE YOUR THOUGHT PATTERNS AND FEELINGS, OBSERVING AND UNDERSTANDING YOUR DEEP SELF AND WHERE IT COMES FROM.
TECHNICAL SYSTEMS TO ESTABLISH A NEW PARADIGM, ALONG WITH A FEELING OF INTIMATE SATISFACTION ALMOST IMMEDIATELY, AND MAINTAIN IT, HACKING YOUR BRAIN REWARD SYSTEM AND ALLOWING YOU, TO GET YOU WHERE YOU WISH TO BE, BUT ALSO AND MOST IMPORTANTLY, ENJOYING THE PROCESS.

ROUND OF THANKS:

I would like to thank every one that is been near me in the period of the writing, in particular Naomi ,Peppa, Susanna, Carla, Zac, Raffael, Shane, Luciana, Teresa, Isabel, Andrew, Lawrence, Gemma, Nick, Laura, Marie, Katrine and Reece; I guess they know why... I say for they support and help... Of course I would like to thank my parents Anna e Raimondo, my family and friends... I would also like to thank who was not near, because I love you ether way, I love you even when you are absent, unconditionally.

About the author: The important thing is the message, not the messenger.

Introduction

It takes a conscious decision to be happy. Sure everyone of us have plenty of reasons to be happy, just we are sometimes more prone to observe the reasons to be unhappy, concentrating our thought and feelings to amplify this last ones, rather than be grateful with what we are and have, and be happy.
I am not saying here, that you should not be ambitious, and dream and plan a better life; just saying, that would not be, probably, a bad idea, to start from happiness, rather than wait for happiness to come when you will achieve your goals.
Easy said than done, be happy.
Is it really possible to take a conscious decision, take a stand, and be happy? Well, you are reading this book to demonstrate yourself so, I did demonstrate myself so. I Have been interested in the subject of self development since my early years of adulthood; I am a 30 years old guy, by the way, at the time of the writing of this book, and I have been studying and researching the subject of self development for the last 9 years, in every form available out there, but also inside myself, in my mind, my feelings, my thought patterns, my habits, and so on; tracking them back to where they came from, I am here to show you, if you like to, how to take a conscious decision to be happy.
I will give you the tools, to be unwired and rewired to be happy, and virtually (and in reality is up to you), obtain and be anything you set up to be in life.
Classical teaching on self development are very much concentrated on goal setting; decide who you want to be, by a date that you set for yourself, then work

out a plan step by step to get there.
Some teaching are practical, They teach you how to follow and study other successful people that have reached the goal you aim to, and do what they do.
Other teaching are more mystical, and are based on the law of attraction, they tell you how to focus yourself on what you really want, and feel like you have already obtain the result , and the result will find his magical way to get to you.
The problem with this sort of teachings are multiple;
To analyse the first one, you can indeed do what other successful people do, and obtain their results, but every human been is different and does things in a different way, every brain and mind run in different ways.
Usually successful people do things in a certain way, because they are wired in a certain way; their brains and minds and all their personality is wired in a certain way; if in the other hand, we are not wired that way, even simple things they do, can feel really difficult to EMULATE.
UNTIL we understand OURSELF in the deep, to then be able to remodel and REWIRE ourself to our liking.
The other downturn of the first way of teaching is that you are constantly thinking at the end goal, and projecting your mind on how you will be happy when you will achieve the goal; rather than be happy in this moment, you envision you future happiness.
I will say again (I like to repeat myself, repetition is the mother of skills), nothing wrong on dreaming a better future, just does not seems a bad Idea to start to be happy right now on this present moment, yes, right now if you wish to follow my advice make a list of everything that you are grateful for, things you already have,

not things you will gain in the future.

To envision yourself happy with things you will gain in the future it may be really frustrating, like a donkey chasing a carrot, and overwhelming, delusional, fighting with our natural reward system, instead of having him by our side with gratitude and rewards for our gratefulness; every morning is a gift, every cuddle from our love ones is a gift, every step we are able to make with our legs is a gift, every meal thanks to the farmers and their work, if we do not want to mention God, is not a spiritual book, obviously between the lines you can spot my spiritual traits, but this book is an hand for everyone, believers or not. Just believe on what you have and are, and be thankfully and happy for it.

That sort of attitude of been overexcited for something we do not have, can collide with our reward system; yes keep performing tasks that do not lead to a reward may cause pain and frustration, and ultimately people to give up on their dreams, START FROM HAPPINESS IN THE OTHER HAND IS A GREAT TOOL TO UNDERSTAND AND UNLEASH A GREAT POWER FOR YOU AND EVERYONE AROUND YOU.

The second teaching, and most basic principle, based on the law of attraction, require you to kid with yourself, to be delusional. No plan to follow in here, just establish a belief the you have already achieve the goal you want to reach, and goal will find his magical way to you.

This sort of thinking as well may lead to excess of euforia , which is doom to turn into very painful frustration and unsatisfying feeling, and very likely, that eventuality, the goal will not be reached by the deadline time.

Sometimes the disappointment is so strong that

lead people to give up on their dreams and goals, especially if they have been in the rollercoaster a few times; I have been in there plenty of times.

My approach is different, and it did indeed worked for me. Whatever are your dreams and ambitious, take a stand right now, and take a conscious decision to be happy, I am pretty sure that you have plenty of reasons to be happy.

My promise to you is to give you all the tools to keep your happiness, and grow it exponentially, eventually also getting to your dreams and goals, but enjoying the process.

Chapter 1
What happiness is about?

Happiness is about, from my point of view, to be happy with what we have right now in front of us, with who we are and what we have.
If we do not like what we are and what we have , it is completely possible to change ourselves with what we want to be, and the process could be really quickly.
I am telling you, you can unwire and understand yourself, your feelings, your thought patterns, and understand where they come from, and trough reason and repetition, understand the lessons from negative feelings, and remember the joy of the good moments, in order to rewire yourself to be the magnificent been I believe you were born to be.
Be grateful for all the amazing things we have is really important, sometimes we just go forward like a broken disk, repeating the same broken unhealthy thought patterns.
I am going to show you, how to unwired those last ones, and rewire new ones, full of joy and fulfilment, if you follow me, you will see :)
But first learn to be happy with what you are and have; if you have not made your list of thanks yet, as I advise, now is the time to do so. You will have a feeling of satisfaction right away, just think, and feel; you know what you are and have, make sense of it, no need for suffer. We are all here to help each other and serve one another; we are going to cover the law of service in the last chapter.
So is it really possible to take a stand and be happy? yes Sir, Yes Mam.

Only when you start to be naturally happy, and thankful, and in full joy of what you already have and are; you can then be ready to reprogram your subconscious mind, and rewire yourself.

Yes we are going to need to team up conscious and subconscious mind; remember your subconscious mind is in control most of the time, yep, in an autopilot mode; we need to train our subconscious mind, through conscious repetition on how to be happy, and run the thought patterns we want.

The subconscious mind does follow our orders, and our thought pattern especially when charged with feelings. Let us imagined that feelings have got a magnetic charge and thought have got an electric charge, together they give birth to the electromagnetic field, that is not science, I am not a scientist, it is just imagination, my personal use of a very powerful technique to rewire the brain and mind.

Let us call it PNL, in Italian (programmazione neuro linguistica); what it does mean? it is the use of imagination to reprogram thought pattern and feelings; you can research yourself the subject if interested.

Let us give colour to our newly created electric thought field, which is positively charged: Turquoise.

Let us give colour to our newly created magnetic field, feeling, which is negatively charged: fucsia.

We will comeback to this, in chapter 3 and 4... Unwired & Rewired.

To go back to our current chapter, think of it, it is quite easy to be happy. I will give you all the tools but think of it. Sure there is people that have less than you, so why we are more prone to observe people that have more than us? It is not a bad thing to have dreams and

goals,
but it is even better to stop been jealous of people that have more than us, and feel compassion for the people that have less, and why not, start to give something when we can. To give start the process of to get; it is like a game words: like forgiveness...
To give pardon, to get peace; forgive to forget;
for give pardon, to forget our bad feelings, for get peace.
forgive others and ourself may be the second step to be happy; I forgive in autopilot, but you may want to take a look at some people you may have to forgive, or it may be even just yourself, we will look more in dept at it in chapter 3 which deal with unwiring ourselves.
Happiness is about reward system in our brains, which release chemicals, when we are doing the best we can in any given moment; to name a few: dopamine, serotonine, endorphins... For example endorphins get released after a run, yes jogging, which is good for our body.
Dopamine get realised when we performe a task we had set up to perform, like when we accomplish our to do list.
Serotonine get realised when we spend time with our loved ones.
The reward system is mostly involved with dopamine, which is a vital chemical, that helped us through out all evolution; in fact our brains a wired for survival, but now days, distractions and consumer society it is a different ambient altogether, this divergence between our wiring and the ambient around cause us stress.
But surly now days we have the information technology and power to unwire and rewire ourselves, even

more in the future; But bare with me, already now!!!
So, what happiness is about? For everyone of us is about a different thing, a different story, everyone of us have their own version of success and happiness in their mind as dreams or goals.
If you are reading this book, I may guess, that you are interested in the field of self development, and or you may be looking for happiness; well guess what, happiness is right in your hands; this book for you should already be happiness; if you are reading this book, likely you have money for food, for clothes, money to buy this book, so you already are rich in terms of money.
Consumer Society tell us we need much more, we are jealous of what other people have and are.
We did cover already that jealousy is not a good feeling, and it does go hand to hand with limiting thought patterns and beliefs: we are not enough, we have not enough; all lies we are sort of addicted to tell to us, because if we are happy, what is there left to look forward to?
Well, more happiness, a steady growth of happiness. Everyone of us go trough life with up and downs; well, we should search for less up and downs and a more steady grow of happiness, joy, gratefulness and fulfilment with ourselves and with others, there is always someone there, looking to share his or her joy with us, if we look forward to share our joy with them.
it is like the imaginary electromagnetic field we spoke about; it does attract people with similar thought patterns and feelings...

Chapter 2
Why I am who I am? Why I do what I do?

Well, some field in psychology, teach us, that we pick up patterns from our surroundings, early in our childhood, from family, teachers, ambient; where we are born and where we grew up.
What patterns? Thought patterns and feelings, trait of our personality; what make us who we are.
Yes it is partially genetic code, but as neuroscience as proven, our brain it is not fixed hard wired, but his plasticity can be remodel with proper training, which you are going to get, exactly here, from this book.
The brain is continuously changing, trough experience and or, as we are going to do; training.
Our experience and our perception of the world, constantly change who we are.
The problem is, that often, human beens, keep repeating the same broken disk in their minds, and even worse they attach to it a negative emotional charge; yes, I may be confusing you, right now (but remember my PNL it is fantasy and not science), emotional charge can be negative or positive.
It is a battle between love and hate, it is you really you, or it is you really fake.
Human beens use to carry thought patterns and feelings from the early years of childhood.
When we are kid we are like sponges, absorbing from our surrounding; than we keep the patterns and feelings continuously changing, trough out our life, in autopilot, trough experiences; does not have to bee that way, we can change our patterns and feelings base in

our liking, as long as we like what we have.
That is all, like what you have, and it will be given even more, I remember someone saying something like this trough out my training.
Do not worry, I will give you the tools to rewire yourself to be anything you set up to be in life.
Just first take a stand, a conscious decision, and be happy!! Repetition is the mother of skills; remember to be grateful for what you have and you are: a magnificent been with 5 and likely more senses, remember your family and friends, your job, your partner, if you have one.
I just broke up with who could have been the woman of my life, a beautiful lady; I am not devastated by this, only because I always leave the door open for the unexpected, I do recognise my mistake by the way and I try to learn from them; but we are not here to talk about my personal life.
I am here to serve you, and, who knows, maybe to serve myself too, serving you.
Remember is not important the messenger but the message.
So you may find in yourself traits from your father or mother, or something you picked up from a school teacher, or your friends; well you keep picking up.
They say you are the sum of the people you allow to enter your space and your life; it does not have to be that way, you can be completely in charge of who you are and you want to be, just bare with me.
Remember the neuroplasticity of you brain allow you to reshape your synaptic connections trough experience, or most importantly trough training; that is what you are doing here with me: learning how to retrain your

brain, allow birth of new neurons, and a new rewiring connections between them, with neurotransmitter and chemicals, but all already available in our body system; we just need to give the conscious order trough repetition (of course if you not suffer of mental disease, in the case medicine and technology it is here to help too).

Yes we seem to be stepping up on chapter 4, which is rewired, but we are not, we are following a process and by now the process is already started and trough repetition you should be already another person, so, who are you? I am an happy guy or girl, or whatever you want to call yourself.

For example: I am Luca and I am Happy, I am so grateful for everything I am and I have (I have made my personal list several times).

If needed write down your list of thanks for, everyday from scratch, repeat, repeat, repeat...

Repetition is the mother of skills...

Repeat even multiple times per day.

Do not kid with your mind on how you would be when achieve your goals.

Be happy with what you are and have right now; that is the starting point: happiness, get rid of limiting belief. You are perfect the way you are, and with you have got right now, even if you in fact are short of 1 or plus senses, you should know by researching un the web, that everything is in the process of getting created if not already created.

Be happy with what you are and have, but know that you will healthy grow your happiness exponentially, with less and less up and downs; an healthy steady grow. You can research on the web and also inside your self where your thought patterns come from, understand them, making sense of them, spoil them, rewire and defeat those ones you do not like.

Training will be here provide, but I have to be completely honest with you, this is the pinnacle of my research, you will have to do your own work on yourself; not hard working, but rather smart working.

If you have made a few researches when advise , you now you should be already on the path of unwiring and rewiring yourself.

The only time you will have is now, past and future are only projection of ourself in our minds;

Neuro science has proven that our brain keep changing our memories based on our wiring. So, it is better to be wired to enjoy good memories; what do you think?

even if you have a recording video of something happens it is still now days almost impossible to remember the exact feelings we had; we can project our future, but we should be flexible in order to not follow into ups and downs, every day it will be something to look forward, something to be grateful for, you are going to (if you so wish), to rewire yourself for more and more up and less down.

But even the downs will only be insightful lesson, not felt as negative experience... Just experience and lessons; We are now stepping up in the next chapter, but remember repetition is the mother of skills.

This little book is setup to really help everyone, and also me of course, I guess I am part of the one, everyone. Yes I would love to make some money out of it and be financially free, I think I deserve it, but is trough the low of service that we will cover in the last chapter , that the real magic happens.

I give a few glimpse here and there about my personal live, to give an input.

I forgive myself for what happened, I do try to learn my lessons and be more and more in peace with my new version of myself; Not such things as failure, or we are successful or we learn lessons.

This little book is setup to be easy to read for everyone, people into self development should know most of the thing I am talking about, but I am making it easy (as much as I can), for everyone to understand.

My techniques are simple and easy to perform and yet so powerful, just bare with me.

It is really a paradox paradigma life changing, from a little book, so much knowledge, it is really to know the edge you have got against the consumer society; sure we do are part of the consumer society, we just need a balance and a new rewiring...

Science and math predictions say that in a few decades we will merge with artificial intelligence, then would all be much more easy to understand and rewire ourself; but still now day, we are ready for happiness.

Think of it, even the simple act to be able to pick up our phones and video call our love ones, where ever we are and where ever they are, it is a gift from the technologies company so criticised, or from God? From the universe? Call it what you want, but is a gift; and so is life, we should be grateful for it since is not earned, we did not designed life (or a list yet, ahahah), it is a gift, which we should honour and be grateful for.

By now you are thinking all chapters are entangled? Yes they are as are all the wiring in your brain, that is me unwiring my understanding on How I have achieve happiness, for you; not much wrote until know right? Well bare with me, it is all here between the lines; seek and you should fine; also we will be leveraging technology and much more, leveraging time, leveraging habits, leveraging the law of service, and much, much much more...

Of course you can then research your own knowledge (KNOW your EDGE).

We are in the era of the information, also it is a possibility that you already have been studying a lot of self development and this is the pinnacle and key to your happiness, I very much belief in so, if that is you, you are one of my favorite targeted customers, at the end of this book you may realise that you were blind, and know you see.

So, why I am what I am? Why I do what I do?

Limiting belief are usually the problem, picked up from our environment, from early childhood, and then again less and less trough experience and people surrounding us, the subconscious mind is in charge in autopilot.

Limitless rewiring technique cooperating with conscious and subconscious mind, trough repetition in this book may be the solution.

Repetition of reading the book may be needed, repetition of the techniques is essential.

Chapter 3
Unwired

Whenever you feel a problem, or an unsatisfactory feeling or thought, ask yourself: where does it come from? where is the lesson? usually there is a lesson to be learned; but that is not always the case.
Sometimes it is just a problem out of our control, coming from another human been, or behaviour of another human been...
Ether way, it is a feeling that we do not want with us, usually to a feeling there is always attached a thought, ether conscious or subconscious.
We need to deeply observe ourselves, in 2 levels: our "hard wiring" from childhood and early experience of adulthood and the other experience that kept changing us; but also observe our thoughts and feelings in this present moment.
Trough reason and repetition we are able to rewire ourselves.
We can work on our unwiring in idle time, catching up up for the day.
Remember to solve the problem, and forgive yourself and others.
A technique I like to use, is the shower technique; everyone after work take a shower right? Or a list, I like to think that...
while in the shower you are getting rid of bacteria and sweat, get also rid of negative feelings and thought patterns. You can us PNL if you like, seek and you should find, it is a technique I will talk about later on. You may have had for example a particularly stressful working day; reason trough it, is it something you

could have done better? Could you had performe better? If yes learn the lesson for the next time, take a note o how to act the next time, I like to use a big writing board always available in my office.

Forgive yourself for the mistake and be at peace, but keep treasure of the lesson learned.

Sometimes we have no part in the fault, in the origins of our problems, in this case our fault is to keeping having hard feelings towards a certain situation.

In both ways forgive and forget, forgive yourself in the first case and others in the second case, a third time may be that there is need for bought; always try in this case, to have a conversation with the counter part, make your effort, and than see; sometimes, most of the time there is a reasonable conclusion and understanding between the 2 parts; if that does not happen, be a peace forget what happened, find the best solution, keep what needed, but do not let frustration and anger eat up your energy.

It is important to let go of feelings and thought patterns not worth to inhabit our body, just let them go, reason your way why to let them go, then let them go.

You can help yourself with music, with your favorite music you can retune your self or new self, and who knows it may happened you may develop a new taste for new music, but if you do not, not worries, when you listen to you favorite music is the love side of you a live, remember it use to be a battle between love and hate, it is your really you, or it is your really fake.

You may feel as money as a constant problem, ether if you have little or if you have enough and in abundance; likely money is a subject that cause stress; it does not have to be that way; be grateful for what you

have; our old ancestor where grateful and thankful to be able to meet the next meal. Think, just think of the vampire that inhabit your body (thought pattern and feelings) and trough reason get rid of them, do not feed them, get rid of them.
Explain from the conscious mind why it is necessary to get rid of them, and trough repetition you are able to rewire your subconscious mind; attach with this process feelings of joy and peace; peace now is found and you are able to rewire yourself.
Are you starting to feel a change? I mean it may be early, thats a book that can be easily read all at once, but if you are reading on multiple sections, to write another list of thanks right now, may not be a bad Idea.
So, what are you grateful for? have you got your 5 senses? if is not, do not worry technology and medicine are RIGHT NOW taking care of that as well. Remember be grateful for all the big things you have, and also for all the little things that come...
Neuroscience now teach us that when we are 2 years old, we have got far more connections and wiring between our neurons than when we are adults.
We are born as nearly empty vessels with our little blueprint of genetic code, but we are empty vessels; that is what make us human, you see animal are born with nearly all their skills already learned.
Us as human been we absorb like sponges from our environment; a 2 years old has got much more connections than an adult human been, from then on, he or she will start to cancel out wiring to adapt to the ambient around; than we keep changing based on our ambient and our experience, OR WE CAN RETRAIN OURSELVES TO BE WHATEVER WE WANT TO

BE.

Let's not keep repeating the same broken disks, the same thought pattern over and over again, especially when attached to negative feelings.

Reason your way out, and explain to your subconscious why certain patterns are not good, with information, reason and love, your weapon is ready to rewire yourself.

From my point of view we are here for love, to keep in mind our love ones, it is really important; have a nice balance of work life and social activity it is really important, a good nutrition and good exercise it may be important as well.

Good nutrition and exercise are far less costly than bad nutrition and laziness.

To cook a good meal takes less money than buy already cooked unhealthy food.

Exercise can be done even at home for free, or nearly; well a connection to the web is needed, but who now days haven't got it ?! So exercise can be done even for free, following youtube videos.

In order to rewire ourselves we need to unwire and understand what is holding us back, where we took the limiting belief from; for some of us maybe only some procrastination holding us back; here is where discipline is required.

Master the skill to show up, show up to your to do list made the night before, and you will see the inspiration and motivation will come.

Someone once said: actions became habits and habits become your destiny.

Chapter 4
Rewired

So here we are, rewiring ourselves, remember: repetition is the mother of skills.
What we can do is to use PNL on our advantage, and swap old thought patterns with good ones we want to rewire; for example, right now, on the time of the writing I am quitting smoking.
My old thought pattern was to want a cigarette, now I am rewiring it to what I need, and I am afraid to say, but what I need is money.
Using PNL, when I think of old thought pattern that I want to swap, I put in my mind an image; on this case the pattern is a desire for me to light up a cigarette, I swap it with a pattern of having enough money to not be worried again about money.
I use PNL based on my personal fantasy.
I swap the cigarette with an image in my mind of a orange tridimensional sfere with geometric rhombuses with angles of 45 degrees (3 D) running counterclockwise, (make sense the colour orange of lighting up a cigarette); with my new image "thought pattern" of having enough money to not be worried again; the same sfere but running clockwise and with colour between dark turquoise and light turquoise.
The technique I have just describe is very powerful for me, because automatically implied repetition, every time I think about lighting up a cigarette I can use the technique to swap my thought pattern and feeling of desire.
Just I do not stay stuck with the desire of money,

because I am enough happy with what I am and I already have.

I can, and you can too, stack up thought patterns and images with arrow and schemes, using PNL.

 example: from the turquoise sfere I attach a sea green arrow, with me virtually writing down my book in the office in colour purple; that would be for me a way to make money, by serving all of you reading and myself too; we will come back to the law of service in the last chapter.

You can stuck up with a scheme and arrows how many patterns you want.

Some times you may need a reason to override old thought patterns; in this case you will have to repeat reasoning out your way out of a pattern or a feeling; first you should recognise why a feeling is coming up, than trough reason move your way out of it, to a solution and a new thought pattern and attached feeling you want to rewrite (rewire).

Eventually trough repetition you will see the miracle happening, old thought patterns and feelings will show up less and less, and new thought patterns and feelings arise.

You will see old thought patterns (broken disk, donkey chasing a carrot) coming up less and less, and lasting less and less, until they will disappear; a this point a new thought patterns will be established; this can happen ether with PNL or without.

Another technique I use, is that one of swapping watch, from the side I usually put my watch (left), to the other side.

Of course I have got an habit to look to the left side for my time right now, but now I attached to left side the thought pattern and feeling of my ex girlfriend leaving me (let's calling in my imagination, electromagnetic field, remember I am not a scientist, but I did studied what I can call mind stuff and did made good use of my imagination, I also did deeply observed myself, unwired myself and rewired myself); now I will have to turn to right side to have a look at the time, on the right side I have got a beautiful girlish watch with some of my favourite colours, and a pink heart ticking the seconds.

My new electromagnetic field is looking for an amazing, beautiful, astonishing girl, inside and outside. I know in my heart she will be there for me, the little heart is ticking. I am ok myself, I do enjoy my company, but I also know I would love to share the love and the live with the one... The one for me...

By the way the watch technique I have created it myself. Coming back to the cigarette technique, I am here just giving some examples, use your amazing imagination, look at you habits, and decide which one is to go and which one is to stay.

You can also swap new electromagnetic fields, I explain myself, I may have the fortune and the pleasure to bring to reality not having to be worry again about money, while still desiring to smoke, I can now connect the desire to a new thought pattern and feeling.

Neuroscience tell us, that after an injury is more easy to rewire your brain; it may and it must be cause of a routine broken, and a new routine can now arise. Remember repetition is the mother of skills, but it is also a double edge sword.

Stop repeating broken disks, get yourself some new enjoyable ones, eventually we may get to a level to have every day a new disk; a fresh new awesome day to enjoy, full of joy and gratefulness.

Remember, do not get yourself bog down if you fail a few times; they success is just a repetition of failures and light at the and of the tunnel of learning, from your failure; remember to always look at the light. Be happy for who you are and you have right now, just be, be happy.

Every single action towards your new self it' s a victory of his own.

Yes, someone said, action become habits, habits becomes your destiny.

You will be amaze to discover how a simple action, a simple showing up to a new habit and thought pattern, tick the needle astonishing, powerfully, like magically, towards your new self, just belief and be, be yourself, be your new self, do the best you can in every single moment and when you cannot, do not field guilty, life is up and downs, but you decide your direction.

Your direction is toward the best version of yourself.

You are already the best version of yourself; well, you are the best version of yourself so far in time; if you are not, just decide, and be, be the best version of yourself, be the best you can, and feel thankful for the lessons when you cannot be, sadness may arise, but this book is your gun, fight and conquer your happiness!!!

Ups and downs should not be a rollercoaster, should be a steady grow of happiness...

Me myself a found my balance, I do wish with all my heart, you to find yours. Bless you.

Chapter 5
Leveraging Technology

Now days we have got beautiful technology available, we not really truly understand the treasure we have; what we know for sure, is, that most of the time, we use it for the wrong reasons, or we just not take enough advantage of it; you see, for example, you are reading my book because of the amazing service amazon offered to me; I am able to express my self, serve you, and who knows, by serving you I may be serving myself too.
Our phones for example are an amazing tool, they are little computers in our hands, in our eyes, in our ears... yes they are our enhances senses already now days.
Phones are also much more, think at the music, our personalised tastes of music directing streaming to our head with our headphones.
You are a good point on rewiring yourself, get rid of old music with words that get you attached to old thought patterns.
Look for new songs reasoning with your new self, attache to them good thought patterns and feelings.
Of course you can keep listening the music you love, if that bring you new feelings of happiness, or the good ones you don't want to get rid of...
In this case attache new thought and feelings to your favourite track songs... Now you are getting to the next level... That is the beginning of technological singularity. Technological singularity it is a term use to describe the merging of machines with human beens, they think it will happen around 2045.
Don't worry, you can decide to keep the all of your

humanity, for now, what I am suggesting is to take advantage of you phone, to rewire yourself; for example using the 3 techniques I am going to describe: calendar technique, alarm technique and wallpaper technique. Our phones keep popping up in windows, directly to our conscious and subconscious the notifications we choose to have.

You can use the calendar to set up a plan to get you where you want to be and keep you disciplined, remembering your plan and tasks for the day.

You can use your calendar to pop up a key word that attache you to a thought pattern and feelings; or you can use both, attaching new thought pattern and feelings with your new routine and or activities; even if you don't show up to perform your task, the window that pop up in your phone, is already reprogramming your subconscious anyway, ether way, not as good as perform a task, but, getting there.

The alarm technique is where you write down the most important task for the day to come, the night before, of course in your phone.

The wallpaper is where your eyes fall all the time you have got the phone in your hand, that as to be the most important goal you have got right now.

Let's make an assumption that your pattern is the most important thing in your life, do not give her or him for granted, there is nothing less appealing to assume him or her will always be there even if we do not water our love everyday.

In that assumption, you would put your beautiful pattern as a wallpaper and a reminder on your calendar every day, repeating, to do something to make her or him happy, also with te reminder to allocate the time for the task; does not have to be always big things, it can be to cook her favorite meal (I am a etero mail, no discrimination for other orientation), or to buy her some flower... Maybe once a month you want to take her out, or once a week, or twice a week ... I do not know your personal finance.. But we do come to manage personal finance to, in the chapter to follow.

Also if you are single looking for a pattern there is apps out there in the web that helps you just do that.

Let's talk about knowledge, full of free knowledge out there in the web, of course check your sources... But just saying, we live in our amazing world, we just have to open our eyes in the morning and be conscious of it.

If you wake up in the morning and you are not happy, take a stand, take a conscious decision, this book as a gone, and be happy.

My book is a little book, can be read even every day, remember, repetition is the mother of skills.

Chapter 6
Personal finance

People usually view money as a problem, no matter if they have got not enough or too much.
usually people with not enough money grew up in an environment with parents or teachers with limiting belief, eventually passed over to the kids; belief such us rich people is greedy, money does not grow on trees, is required to work hard for money.
Well as far as I am aware is required to work smart for money.
Indeed there is rich people greedy, but there is also rich people very much into social activity and dedication to the service of the others, thanks to them we are evolving, but we will come back to the law of service in the last chapter.
I do not want to talk about the ambient I grew up about money, I like to keep my privacy, and remember, is not important the messenger, but the message; but I use to think I did not had enough, and in fact I always found myself without enough; subconsciously believing I did not had enough, made act in a way to lose money to use money out of true reasons, and in fact be without enough money.
I found out I had enough money when I decided I did, in fact with calculation and budgeting technique, I realise I had all the money I needed, for everything and more.
Not saying here to not dream of a better future, just saying would probably not be a bad idea to organise yourself and start to enjoy your freedom, because the cage is only in your mind, no shortage in the outside; the shortage if any, is only inside.

It is easy, just think at all your expanses and put them down in paper, yes think on paper.

Once you have got all your outgoing, think what to prioritise, there is enough money for everything.

I will make an example, here is my last plan, I made when I was an oldest version of myself, working as a head chef in a restaurant:

First take out the fix bills: rent or mortgage if you got any, electricity, water, council tax, all your fix bills; what is left is the 100 % of your money left.

The 100 % of what you got left you split it up in percentage of what is most important for you.

Example:
-Groceries
-Bathroom products
-Presents
-Celebrations
-Holidays
-Debt repayment (if you got any, get rid first of that one that charge the most higher percentage of interest, but, if your mind is fine with debt, get rid of that one that give you the most burden to your mind; for example, I would pay first de debt with my parents having enough money, and I would put a deposit down to buy an house here in uk; I have already in my mind the ideal real estate).
-Rainy day
-Going out
-Accessories.

Now you have got to prioritise; think at your expanses, and prioritise the most important things to you; think how much you usually spend for every voice; if you think well enough, you will find out, there is enough for everything.

Now you just have to be disciplined.
example:
Once I took out my fix bills, and my groceries, 27 % goes in savings, what is left is divide in percentage like that:
-Presents 6 %
-Celebrations 4 %
-Holidays 30 %
-Debt repayment 10 %
-Rainy day 10 %
-Going out 30 %
-Accessories 10 %
We now have the all 100 %.
Now is a matter of doing the calculations when the money come, and be disciplined, respecting the budget. Remember, I am not asking to not dream and plan a better future; just suggesting that would not be a bad idea, to start right now, from happiness. You can always plan and dream a better future, just start right now from happiness.

Chapter 7
Health, nutrition, exercise

Health is the most important thing we have got; well, love should be the most important thing we have got, just there is not love without health; unless we are talking about sick love, well that is not good.
Health start in our mind, yes, it start in our subconscious, and it is our job to train our subconscious for health and abundance.
We are required to train our subconscious mind, to show up to the programs we are rewiring.
For example we may be rewiring a program to go to run, or to exercise, or to eat healthy.
To eat healthy give us the proper nutrition balance needed for our body to perform as the best it can; mediterranean diet is the most healthy diet on the planet, according to doctors and also my own experience, you can research on the web, what it is about.
Eat healthy, start with shopping healthy, you will find out that eating healthy it is also an ally to your wallet: start cooking yourself your own meals if you are not already doing it.
You see, this book give you inputs, but then you will have to do your own research and home work to find your own way.
The techniques I have been showing you, are the techniques I have been using on my own, gives you general ideas, to take a stand, a conscious decision and be happy, but then is up to you to find your own way.
Exercise are very good, for your body and also your mind; for example after a run your brain release

very cool chemicals called endorphins; which make you feel good, like a drug, a very healthy natural drug.

You can find on app stores, application for your phone, to get you start, even if you never have been running in your life; that is another way of leveraging technology for example.

It is important to keep your body as good as your mind is, to be in a happy state of mind.

Another way of leveraging technology is to use youtube exercise video, you see, is not required to you to go to the gym, in order for you to keep your state of mind and body in good health.

It is not required to have a perfect body, you will find your own balance. Just take a stand, a conscious decision, and retrain your subconscious to be happy.

If you read this book, first thing in the morning for 21 days, then you will see it, you will believe it, your subconscious is ready and trained to look for the right answers and make you happy.

Exercise your brain and mind as well not just your body. Your brain is like a mussel, the more you feed it, then more you can feed it.

Feed your brain with the right food, feed your heart with the right food; love is the right food for you heart; do not criticise or judge other people, focus on yourself, look for the good on yourself and others; observe the goodness. hate is fake, do not exist in real life; only exist in the poor minds they feed themselves with.

Chapter 8
Loved ones

The people we love is the essential food for our souls. Yes health and love goes hand in hand.

We should love ourselves first, and then the others, unconditionally, no one is perfect; so we should love ourselves and our partners, family and friends, unconditionally.

The beautiful feeling of love is at the core of our very essence, it is life himself, or herself; life does not have a gender, so does not love.

I am not talking of romantic love, that can be or cannot be, there is not essential needing for that.

There is essential needing to love ourselves and the people around us, unconditionally.

At times may seems difficult to love people unconditionally; just remember forgive and forget; forgive people to get forgiveness and peace; when you forgive they will forgive you. Forgive and forget. Forgive forgiveness, for get, to get, peace of mind and heart.

Do not stay with the same broken disks; also forgive yourself in first person, and try to learn from your mistakes.

Love is at the core of our very essence, that is my view, yes health is on first place, just I do not believe there is health without love, not talking here about sick love, talking about the love for our family whoever they are, it could be friends if not family, or colleagues, or family, or your partner.

If you are lucky enough it may be the all of them; if you are lucky enough do not, please, let your limiting belief tell you you are not happy. Because you already are by now, and you are loved, because I love you, *whoever you are, I love you, did you hear me? I love you, unconditionally.*

Chapter 9
The law of service

You see the law of service is the most important law on this universe, we are all here to serve each other, learn from each other, and love each other.

You may now find out that the people most rich of money, is the people that served the most other people, a few examples: Bill gates, Jeff Bezos ... They gave us amazing services; you see nothing happens by coincidence. Do you want to be rich ? Think, how can you serve? what value can you bring to the market? Keep moving for yourself and for others.

Do not think at the house complete, put down the brick in the best way you can, right now.

Do the thing you love to do, listen to your favourite music, go in holiday to your favourite place, you now know you have got enough money.

It is allow to dream and plan a better future; what value can you bring to the market? How can you be of service to others?

Writing this book I hope I have been of service to you, and by been of service to you, I have been of service to myself too. I love you, whoever you are, whatever mistake have you been making in the past. I love you unconditionally. I wish you happiness: read this book first thing in the morning for 21 days; your subconscious will give you the answer you are looking for. That is my promise to you. Your promise to yourself? take a conscious decision, right now!!! be Happy!!

With Love

Luca Muscas

Printed in Great Britain
by Amazon